How to use this book

Follow the advice, in italics, given for you on each page.
Support the children as they read the text that is shaded in cream.
Praise *the children at every step!*

Detailed guidance is provided in the Read Write Inc. Phonics Handbook.

8 reading activities

Children:
- *Practise reading the speed sounds.*
- *Read the green, red and challenge words for the story.*
- *Listen as you read the introduction.*
- *Discuss the vocabulary check with you.*
- *Read the story.*
- *Re-read the story and discuss the 'questions to talk about'.*
- *Re-read the story with fluency and expression.*
- *Practise reading the speed words.*

Speed sounds

Consonants *Say the pure sounds (do not add 'uh').*

f	l	m	n	r	s	v	z	sh	(th)	ng
ff	(ll)				ss	(ve)	zz			nk
							s			

b	c	d	g	h	j	p	qu	t	w	x	y	(ch)
bb	k		gg						wh			tch
	(ck)											

Vowels *Say the vowel sound and then the word, e.g. 'a', 'at'.*

at	hen	in	on	up	day	see	high	blow	zoo

*Each box contains one sound but sometimes more than one grapheme. Focus graphemes are **circled**.*

Green words

Read in Fred Talk (pure sounds).

then   this   off   much   back   pink   just

lost   wet   that   big   sun   have   will

Read the root word first and then with the ending.

fit → fits

Red words

said   to   the   go   I   she   now

play*   my*   too*

* Red word for this book only

Vocabulary check

Discuss the meaning (as used in the story) after the children have read the word.

definition:

sun hat   *a hat with a brim to keep the sun off your face*

Punctuation to note in this story:

Max Mum	*Capital letters for names*
Put Much This	*Capital letters that start sentences*
.	*Full stop at the end of each sentence*
!	*Exclamation mark used to show anger and surprise*

Go and play

Introduction
Do you like watching TV? Max does, even when it's a nice sunny day. His mum wants him to go outside and play. She tells him to turn the TV off and find a sun hat. Max says he's lost it, but he doesn't want to wear anyone else's sun hat instead!

Story written by Cynthia Rider
Illustrated by Tim Archbold

"Put that TV off,"
said Mum.

"Put on a sun hat and
go and play."

"I have lost my sun hat," said Max.

"Put on Dad's sun hat then," said Mum.

"Much too big!" said Max.

"Put on my sun hat then," said Mum.

"Much too pink!" said Max.

Mum got Jack's sun hat.

"This fits," she said.
"Now, go and play!"

"Much too wet!"
said Max.

"I will just have to put the TV back on!"

Questions to talk about

FIND IT QUESTIONS
✓ Turn to the page
✓ Read the question to the children
✓ Find the answer

Page 8–9: Why does Max think he can't go out and play?

Page 10: Whose hat is much too big for Max?

Page 11: Whose hat does Max think is too pink?

Page 12: Whose hat fits?

Page 13: Why can't Max go out and play?
Do you think he's disappointed?